Doomsday Scenarios:
Separating Fact from Fiction™

WORLD FINANCIAL MELTDOWN

Laura La Bella

rosen publishing's
rosen
central®

New York

To North Kilian, in hopes that Social Security will still be around when you retire

Published in 2010 by The Rosen Publishing Group, Inc.
29 East 21st Street, New York, NY 10010

Library of Congress Cataloging-in-Publication Data

La Bella, Laura.
World financial meltdown / Laura La Bella.
    p. cm.—(Doomsday scenarios: separating fact from fiction)
Includes bibliographical references and index.
ISBN 978-1-4358-3564-1 (library binding)
ISBN 978-1-4358-8530-1 (pbk)
ISBN 978-1-4358-8531-8 (6 pack)
1. Financial crises. 2. International finance. I. Title.
HB3722.L3 2010
338.5'42—dc22

                                                              2009021090

Manufactured in Malaysia

CPSIA Compliance Information: Batch #TWW10YA: For Further Information contact Rosen Publishing, New York, New York at 1-800-237-9932

On the cover: A trader working on the floor of the New York Stock Exchange has a stunned reaction to the steep fall of stocks in September 2008.

CONTENTS

Introduction

If you have a bank account, imagine stopping by the ATM one afternoon to take out some money so that you can go grocery shopping. You enter your bank card, punch in your PIN, and wait. Instead of requesting the amount of money you need, the ATM tells you that you no longer have access to your money. You don't think much of it, since ATMs can break down. Knowing that you have your credit card, you go to the grocery store to make a purchase. You step up to the register and scan your card. But nothing happens. Your card no longer works either. You have no way of making a purchase or getting access to your money in the bank.

Feeling scared and uncertain, you return home and turn on the television. The news reports are shocking. The U.S. banking system has frozen and is on the brink of collapse. The world economy is crumbling. ATM cards are useless, credit cards no longer work, and getting your money out of the bank—well, good luck. You turn on your computer in an attempt to access your bank's Web site. You are shocked to see

S&P 1197.06 ▼ 54.64 | DOW 10947.15 ▼ 474.84 | NAS 2179.91 ▼ 81.36

COVERAGE.
CRUDE OIL TONIGHT DOWN

WALL ST Crisis:

IS YOUR MONEY SAFE?

SPECIAL REPORT 7 - 9P

LIVE COVERAGE FROM CNBC

9 - 11P ET

First Trust En... 19.10 ▼ 1.8

After the dramatic fall of the stock market in September 2008, the media reported the steep loss in stock value, and financial analysts began to predict the widespread impact of the event.

that all of your hard-earned money is gone. What are you going to do?

The news networks show major social upheaval taking place in cities around the world. People are stealing food and supplies, and they're breaking into homes to look for money. Mass hysteria has set in. A survival-at-all-costs mentality is building. You no longer feel safe in your own home. Both the police and the military are overwhelmed by the social unrest as violence breaks out all over. People are desperate and scared.

But how likely is it that this disastrous chain of events will really play out in this way? Do we face the inevitability of financial ruin? Or is this just a hyped-up situation, like many other doomsday scenarios, which was created to scare us?

While there is always the potential for financial collapse in any economy, the odds are highly unlikely. We have come close on a few occasions. The Great Depression was a decade-long hardship that affected a generation of people and their spending habits for the rest of their lives. Other countries, including Russia, have seen catastrophic economic collapses, record-high unemployment, and severe poverty. It can happen. We have seen it happen.

However, the United States is one of the most powerful nations in the world and one of the strongest economically. There have been difficult economic times in our history, and there will be again in our future. But an all-out financial melt-down is not a likely doomsday scenario that will spell the end of our economy, as we'll see in this book.

Chapter 1

WHAT IS A DOOMSDAY SCENARIO?

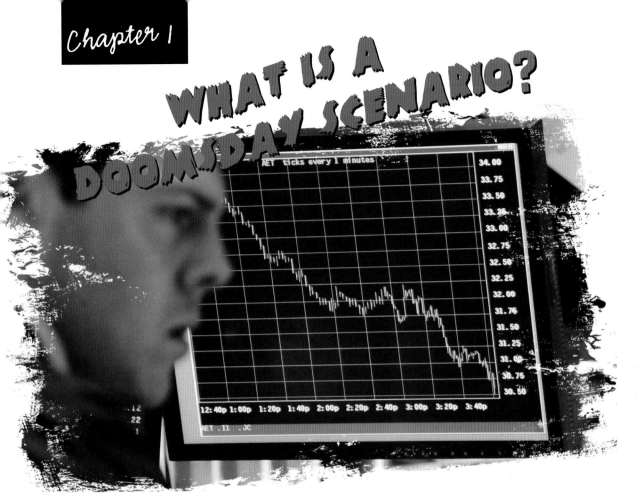

As stock values plunged in 2009, Wall Street's reputation as the financial capital of the world began to crumble. New York City's top financial houses either closed, consolidated, or received government help.

Before we begin to think about the worldwide collapse of our economy and the financial systems that support it, we must first define "doomsday scenario" and understand how one can occur.

A doomsday scenario is a specific event that has an exceptionally destructive effect on the world. Doomsday events include such scenarios as a breakdown in the food supply system, nuclear attacks, deadly viruses, catastrophic climate change, and the collapse of the world financial system. They can range in seriousness from a significant disruption in how we live our daily lives to the extinction of human life. Doomsday scenarios are often global in scope, which means that they affect everyone, everywhere.

A poll by SciFi.com, the Web site of the Sci-Fi television network, revealed that virtually all Americans believe that some sort of doomsday scenario could realistically impact the human race, and many feel that such a scenario is likely to be man-made or influenced.

Doomsday scenarios often fall into three categories: natural occurrences, man-made events, and supernatural events. Natural occurrences might include a global pandemic, a geological event (such as a volcano or massive flooding), or severe climate change caused by the natural cycle of the earth and the sun. Man-made events are those that are influenced by the decisions made by humans. These events might include nuclear, chemical, or biological war; the depletion of oil and other natural resources; and severe global warming caused by our abuse of the environment. The third category is supernatural events. Supernatural events are highly unlikely occurrences that are associated with mythology or religious judgments.

What Is an Economic Collapse?

While we discuss the hypothetical scenarios for how human life on Earth may come to an end, we need to look beyond these scary, yet unlikely, scenarios. As we have experienced before in our nation's history, economic collapse can have a global impact on our lives. It also presents a more realistic end to human civilization than other, more fantastical endings, such as a black hole sucking the planet into oblivion, an asteroid impacting the earth, or an alien invasion.

An economic collapse is the devastating breakdown of our international, national, or regional economy. It is essentially a severe economic depression distinguished by a significant number of businesses going bankrupt and massive unemployment. A full or near-full economic collapse is often quickly followed by months, years, or even decades of economic depression, social chaos, and civil unrest.

An economic collapse, however, is much different from an economic disaster resulting from natural causes. For example, when Hurricane Katrina slammed into the Gulf Coast in April 2006, the storm's devastation reached much further than the destruction of homes and property. The storm destroyed thirty oil platforms, forced the closure of nine oil refineries, and interrupted the country's oil supply. The storm also destroyed the Gulf Coast's highway infrastructure and disrupted the export of products, such as grain. Hundreds of thousands of local residents were left unemployed. Thousands of homes were completely submerged in floodwaters that rose 20 to 30 feet (6 to 9 meters) high. Thousands of people were forced to leave New Orleans and the surrounding areas after the levees broke and flooded the city. Many ended up leaving permanently when the recovery and rebuilding effort was slow to begin.

However, even amid the wide-scale destruction, the closing of businesses, and the poor response, recovery, and rebuilding effort, the U.S. economy was largely uninterrupted. While people were affected nationally by rising gas prices, the storm did not hurt employment on a national scale. The storm's effects were mostly felt in the Gulf Coast area, which include the states of Texas and Mississippi. The area struggled to recover.

While Hurricane Katrina might represent a regional economic disaster, widespread economic collapse occurs when there are breakdowns in multiple financial and business systems worldwide. As a result, these breakdowns cause widespread unemployment, higher rates of interest and inflation, and a considerable slowdown in consumer spending. Often, the government gets involved in bringing the economy back from the brink of collapse. However, government aid can often be slow.

The Economic Cycle

There are four basic phases that make up an economic cycle:

- Phase 1: Economic slowdown. The first phase of the economic cycle begins when the economy begins to slow and the demand for products is not as high.
- Phase 2: Recession. In phase 2, the economy slows to a point where unemployment rises, production slows or stops, and the economy is at its weakest point.
- Phase 3: Economic recovery. In this phase, the economy is beginning to grow, companies are getting back on track and producing products again, and more jobs become available.
- Phase 4: Expansion. This highest phase of the economic cycle is where we see expansion in many areas of the economy. Lots of jobs are available, companies are working hard to meet the demand for products, people are investing in businesses, and consumer spending is at its peak.

Does History Repeat Itself?

The Great Depression began in 1929 and lasted until about 1939. It was the longest and most severe economic depression ever experienced in the industrialized world. Though the U.S. economy had actually begun to decline six months earlier, the Great Depression began with the stock market crash in October 1929. The collapse of stock market prices ruined thousands of individual investors as they watched

The front page of the *Brooklyn Daily Eagle* carries a stunning headline, "Wall St. in Panic as Stocks Crash." The stock market crash on October 24, 1929, known as "Black Thursday," marked the beginning of the Great Depression.

their assets, or possessions, decrease in value. The crash strained banks and other financial institutions, particularly those holding stocks in their portfolios. By 1933, of the twenty-five thousand U.S. banks, more than eleven thousand were forced out of business.

This, combined with a national loss of confidence in the economy, led to lower levels of consumer spending. With no one buying anything beyond the necessities to live each day, there was no longer a need for the great number of products that were available to the public. Manufacturing slowed and many businesses went bankrupt. The result was a drastically rising unemployment rate. By 1932, U.S. manufacturing production was cut in half and unemployment rose to unprecedented levels of about 25 percent. The United States was not the only country affected, however. The Great Depression was an international economic problem. Cities all around the world were hit hard, especially those dependent on heavy industry.

There have been a number of significant occurrences when the economy, or large parts of it, has collapsed and caused widespread economic problems. Are we doomed to repeat history? There have also been several smaller economic situations that continue to have lasting effects, ones that have occurred more recently than the Great Depression.

The Stock Market Crash of 1987

The stock market crash of 1987, also known as "Black Monday," refers to a series of international events that occurred on Monday, October 19, 1987. On this date, stock

When the stock market crashed on October 19, 1987, traders frantically attempted to sell stocks as panic swelled around the country.

markets around the world, beginning in Hong Kong and spreading through Europe and finally reaching the United States, crashed. Black Monday was the largest one-day decline in the history of the stock market. Heavy stock trading and the overinflated value of stocks were two of the major reasons for the crash.

The most popular explanation for the 1987 crash was selling by program trading, which is the use of computers to perform rapid sales of stock. As computer technology became more available, the use of program trading grew dramatically within Wall Street firms. After the crash, many Wall Street stockbrokers and financial executives blamed the computer programs for blindly selling stocks as the stock market continued to fall, which only made the problem worse.

The Collapse of Savings and Loans

The savings and loan crisis of the 1980s and 1990s, commonly known as the "S&L crisis," was the failure of 747 savings and loan associations in the United States. The problems began when savings and loan managers created several innovations, such as alternative mortgage instruments and interest-bearing checking accounts, as a way to retain funds and generate loans. It all collapsed when the savings and loans associations did not have the money in hand when people wanted to withdraw money from their accounts.

Bursting of the "Dot-com" Bubble in the Early 2000s

By 2000, a million new Web pages were created every day as the popularity and usefulness of the Internet grew. It was

The 2012 Doomsday Prediction

The 2012 doomsday prediction is a cultural phenomenon that forecasts significant, cataclysmic events in the year 2012. The idea is widespread, with a number of books, Internet sites, and film documentaries dedicated to understanding the accuracy of the prediction.

The 2012 doomsday prediction is primarily based on the proclaimed end date of a calendar called the 5,125-year Mesoamerican Long Count calendar. This calendar predicts that on December 21, 2012, we will experience the end of the world. The prediction also includes warnings that the earth will reach an environmental tipping point that could cause mass extinctions. There is also the belief that a number of legends and prophecies, both religious and mythical, will occur.

In addition, some proponents of the 2012 doomsday prediction argue that ancient Mayan astronomers were aware of a rare alignment of the earth, sun, and center of the Milky Way. This alignment is said to occur on the winter solstice of December 21, 2012. According to this belief, the alignment is tied to the precession of the equinoxes and signals a transition from one world age to another. One interpretation of this transition predicts that, during this time, the planet and its inhabitants may undergo a physical or spiritual transformation, rather than an apocalypse.

the peak of the "dot-com" bubble, when countless companies got their big breaks in cyberspace. Dot-coms are companies that do the majority of their business on the Internet. However, the bubble burst when a stock market

A stock analyst's chart shows the dramatic fluctuation of stock values. Analysts use this information to make predictions, understand the impact of the rise and fall of stocks, and make plans on how best to recover from losses.

crash in 2000 forced a number of the dot-coms to go out of business. Thousands of people lost their jobs. Many investors who put up money to help establish these businesses on the Web lost money.

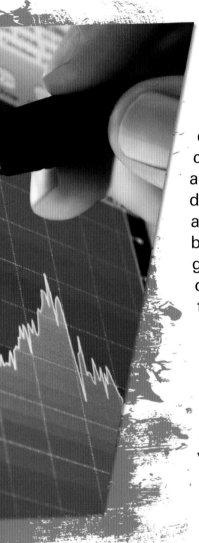

The Economic Cycle

The term "economic cycle" refers to the natural fluctuations in production or economic activity that occur over the course of several months or years. There are periods of growth, or expansion, when demand for products and services is high and companies work to fulfill that demand by increasing their production. These growth periods are followed by a slow-down, when demand falls. Demand can fall too low, and when this occurs, a recession or depression can happen. But each recession or depression is always followed by a recovery period, and the cycle begins again. At one time, business cycles were thought to be regular and highly predictable durations. But today, each cycle can vary in its severity and length.

Chapter 2

CAUSES OF AN ECONOMIC MELTDOWN

There are more than 190 different currencies around the world, including the American dollar, the euro, the British pound, the Chinese yuan, and the Japanese yen.

When we look at doomsday scenarios that could lead to a world financial meltdown, there are only four that hold any kind of legitimacy against the odds that they might actually occur. They include the introduction of a new global currency, a real and significant economic crash, the influence and impact that the country of China has on the United States, and the threat of another major terrorist attack on our nation.

A New Global Currency

There are more than 190 different currencies, or types of money, in the world. Every European nation has its own currency (Switzerland has the franc; England has the pound), as well as a standard form of currency called the euro, which was introduced in 1999. The euro is used by nearly all of the European countries. The Japanese have the yen, and the Chinese have the yuan. But the prevailing currency worldwide is the U.S. dollar. The dollar is the major international reserve currency, which is a form of money that is held in significant quantities by many governments and institutions throughout the world.

A single global currency, called the Terra, has been proposed as a way of simplifying the number of currencies available worldwide. The Terra, or Dey, is an acronym for the three most popular currencies in the world: the dollar, the euro, and the yen. This new currency would be supported by a central bank, which would be used for all transactions around the world, regardless of the nationality of the entities (individuals, corporations, governments, or other organizations) involved in the transaction. The benefits of one global currency are substantial. One global currency could:

- Eliminate the transaction costs related to trading currencies
- Do away with the need to maintain foreign exchange services, which are used to exchange one currency for another
- Eliminate currency failure, which would make foreign investment decisions much easier in emerging economies

But creating a global currency also has significant challenges. For one, a single currency would have a single interest rate. An interest rate is the price a borrower pays to use money that he or she doesn't own. When you take out a loan to buy a car, an interest rate is charged to the loan amount. This is a way that banks and other financial institutions make money. It's also a significant way to boost an economy. If there were one global currency, a region or nation experiencing an economic depression would be unable to use an increase to its interest rate to boost its economy. The reason is that a global currency would mean an increase, or a decrease, in interest rates that would apply to every country worldwide. No one country would be able to increase or decrease interests rates in order to help its individual economy.

In addition to interest rates being an obstacle, there are a number of political barriers. Each nation has its own political system, making it extremely difficult for the world to adopt one common currency. In the present, nations are not able to work together closely enough to produce and support a common currency. There would need to be a high level of trust between many different countries before a true world currency could be created. While there are a number

Amid the economic uncertainty of early 2009, production of gold bars soared. Manufacture increased to twenty-four hours a day, and the wait for the bars went from ten days to two months.

of countries that work well together now— the United States has strong relationships with European nations, as well as with many Latin American nations—many countries are still at odds with one another.

With currency values decreasing, gold has become a popular topic of conversation. Gold used to be a form of currency. But that changed once countries began to adopt paper currency, such as the American dollar. Then gold became an investment. But in times of financial crisis, when paper currency decreases in value, gold maintains or increases its value.

A global currency would cause wide financial collapse in a number of nations and is not a realistic option for the world financial system. This has not stopped nations from proposing the idea or working toward wide acceptance.

A Real Economic Crash

An economic crash is characterized by rampant deflation, which is the lowering of prices over time; 15 percent unemployment; and a 35 percent loss of gross domestic product (GDP). GDP is one of the ways we measure a country's national income and its economy. GDP is the total value of all the goods and services produced in a particular country. The United States is ranked number one for GDP worldwide, followed by China, Japan, and Germany, respectively.

Can an economic crash occur? The simple answer is yes, it can. And it has. The Great Depression is the most severe

The ABC News ticker in New York's Times Square announces the collapse of two major financial firms, Lehman Brothers, which declared bankruptcy, and Merrill Lynch & Co., which was rescued by Bank of America.

economic crash in world history. But a crash of that magnitude is not likely to occur again. However, severe economic crashes will happen as a result of the natural highs and lows of the economy.

The world experienced a severe economic crash in late 2008. At first, the crash appeared to be caused by reckless lending by banks. The crisis originated with a bubble in the residential real-estate market, followed by the inevitable aftermath of declining home prices and a subsequent explosion of home mortgage defaults and foreclosures. In short, these financial institutions loaned money out for mortgages and other purchases, but loans were made to people who were not capable of paying the money back. It soon became clear that the crash was due to a number of factors in addition to poor lending. The resulting losses were worldwide because foreign investors hold enormous amounts of U.S. mortgage-related assets. Financial institutions did not have the capital to absorb these losses. This resulted in the collapse of many of these institutions and the enormous infusion of capital by governments, plus loans and guarantees, to prevent the collapse of many more.

As a result of the financial crisis, a number of large and well-established investment and commercial banks, such as Lehman Brothers and Bear Sterns, suffered massive losses and faced bankruptcy. This led to increased unemployment and signs of other economic downturns in major economies of the world.

A Chinese bank clerk counts RMB, or Renminbi, banknotes at a branch of China Construction Bank. The yuan fell in value in response to the loss of value of the American dollar and stock market prices in 2008 and 2009.

China

There is an urban legend spreading that talks about the chances of a U.S.-China War. The story goes like this: While working for an international corporation, experts on China uncover information about how it intends to launch an attack on the United States. The attack will begin with the Chinese military launching missiles on American military bases in Japan and South Korea, while also launching long-range weapons to destroy American satellites in order to cause a disruption of communications.

In reality, this wartime scenario is pretty far-fetched. However, China does have major influence over the U.S. financial system, and that could spell big trouble for the United States. At the same time, China relies on the American dollar to fuel its own economy. China's growth as a country relies on its sales of goods and services to other countries. Its economy is the second largest in the world after that of the United States, and the United States is very much at the mercy of China when it comes to prices, wages, interest rates, and the value of the American dollar.

The Economic Stimulus Act of 2008

In February 2008, the U.S. Congress passed the Economic Stimulus Act of 2008 to provide several measures intended to motivate the economy, boosting it before it sank further and a recession or depression kicked in. The stimulus package included tax rebates to low-income and middle-income tax-payers; tax incentives to stimulate business investment; the expansion of unemployment benefits and other social welfare provisions; and an increase in domestic spending in such areas as education, health care, and infrastructure (roads, highways, bridges, etc.), as well as investment in the energy industry.

Tensions are rapidly escalating between the United States and China. China owns currency reserves that are worth $2 trillion—two-thirds of which are directly held in U.S. dollars, making it the largest foreign holder of U.S. currency. The American dollar has depreciated, or lost value, over the last several years. As a result, many international banks have begun to diversify, or mix up, the types of currency they have by switching from the American dollar to other currency, such as the euro or yen. This is a big problem for the dollar. First, switching from U.S. assets to European assets causes the dollar to depreciate, making the U.S. dollar less valuable than the currency of foreign countries. Because China holds a significant amount of American dollars, a sudden shift by China to diversify its reserves could potentially cause the dollar to crash, resulting in massive financial problems for the United States.

Terrorism

Terrorist attacks can influence the economy. In places where terrorist activity has been pervasive and protracted, such as Colombia, Northern Ireland, Spain, and Israel, terrorism depresses growth and sometimes stunts economic development. Foreign companies and the money that they would have invested fled Columbia long ago because the country has been beset by drug-related terrorism for more than twenty years. The per-capita income level for this small Latin American nation is now 45 percent below the average. Similarly, when religious violence raged through Belfast in the 1980s and early 1990s, Northern Ireland became the United Kingdom's poorest region as industry and people migrated to the southern republic to escape the terrorist attacks and live in a more secure location.

This Al Qaeda recruitment video is used to entice young people into joining the terrorist organization. The video shows military training tactics that are taught to those who enlist.

Al Qaeda, the terrorist organization responsible for the attacks on the World Trade Center and the Pentagon on September 11, 2001, has long sought to disrupt the U.S. economy. The 9/11 attacks influenced every sector of our

economy. In the days and weeks that followed the attacks, retail sales and travel dropped to significantly low levels. The financial market also struggled to regain its footing. It took several months for these areas of the economy to rebound. But slowly, they did. Retail sales improved. And while the stock market was hit hard immediately after the attacks, it rebounded to pre-9/11 levels within just a few of months.

However, terrorist attacks are complex. They not only cause a loss of human life and often devastating destruction, as witnessed by the collapse of the World Trade Center in New York City, but they also generate widespread fear. Terrorist attacks create a general feeling that we are not safe and perpetuate the fear that more violence is to come. This fear can influence the way that people invest their money, or it can force them to hold back on investing. In addition, the fear of violence often forces companies to spend more money on security. After the 9/11 attacks, many businesses hired more security guards, strengthened their computer security by establishing better firewalls, invested in storage for company records and important paperwork, and took out large insurance policies. This widespread investment in safety took money away from more productive investments, such as employees.

Chapter 3

ECONOMIC MELTDOWN SCENARIOS

In 2009, the United States experienced an increase in unemployment not seen since the Great Depression. Even the most qualified people found it difficult, if not impossible, to get a job.

Chipping away at these financial doomsday scenarios and taking a closer look at each one will give us an idea of what we can realistically expect to happen. Rumor and exaggeration lead to fear and a belief in unlikely scenarios. But looking at the facts and examining the truth will help us determine if our fear is justified and if a threat can become a reality. In this chapter we offer several different financial doomsday scenarios. We'll look at the facts and judge whether or not each situation is a valid potential threat.

Scenario Number One: A Depression Is Coming

Robert Parks, an economist and finance professor at Pace University in New York City, predicted that there was a more than 60 percent probability that financial meltdown in the United States in 2008 would lead to a full-scale depression, much like the Great Depression of the 1930s. Parks believed there would be a steep fall in housing prices, major deficits in the federal budget, a continual decrease in the value of the American dollar, and a weak stock market. Parks believed these things would lead to a depression in which our country would see widespread poverty, rampant loss of homes, unemployment, and even starvation. While Parks was right in guessing that there would be a significant economic situation in 2008, he was wrong about how severe it would become.

Many economists and financial experts thought Parks was wrong. The Great Depression was three times as bad as the economic situation in 2008. During the Great Depression:

- Thirteen million people were unemployed (nationally, the unemployment rate rose to as high as 25 percent).
- Industrial production dropped by 45 percent.
- New home building dropped by 80 percent.
- The stock market lost nearly 90 percent of its value.
- More than one million families lost their farms.
- The average family's income dropped by 40 percent.
- Nine million savings accounts were wiped out.
- Many people, unable to earn an income, went hungry.

In 2008, many companies either closed their doors or significantly cut their workforces. The unemployment rate

31

reached 8.5 percent—a high level for today but a significantly lower rate than what our country experienced during the Great Depression. Experts believed that the economy would slowly turn around; employment numbers would rise to normal levels; and demand would increase for supplies, causing manufacturers to increase their production in order to put more goods into the marketplace.

The U.S. government, in response to the declining economy in 2008 and at the start of 2009, proposed solutions to help the economy get back on its feet. The federal government assisted banks through bailouts, in which the government gives banks money to help cover their debts and loans. A highly detailed infrastructure plan was put into place to improve schools, highways and roads, bridges, and public buildings. The plan would create work from construction companies, which would need to hire additional workers to complete these jobs. The creation of jobs would stimulate the economy because people feel more secure in their personal financial health and begin to spend money again.

Seeds of Change

The Svalbard Global Seed Vault is a storage space buried 400 feet (122 m) inside a mountain in Norway. The Global Crop Diversity Trust maintains the vault, which contains more than 10 tons (10,000 kilograms) of seeds collected from all over the world. More than one hundred million seeds from more than one hundred countries were placed inside the Svalbard Global Seed Vault as a precaution against food scarcity and doomsday scenarios that could cause widespread destruction of agricultural lands.

The Svalbard Global Seed Vault in Norway stores millions of agricultural seeds from around the world that may be used to reestablish the global food supply in the event of a catastrophe.

The purpose of the Svalbard Global Seed Vault is to preserve all of the world's crops. Thousands more plant species will be added as organizers of the Global Crop Diversity Trust attempt to get specimens of every agricultural plant in the world. Their mission is to ensure the conservation and availability of crop diversity for food security worldwide. Even in extreme conditions of global warming, the seeds will be safe for up to two hundred years. Some of the seeds will even be viable for a millennium or more, including barley, which can last 2,000 years; wheat 1,700 years; and sorghum, almost 20,000 years.

Scenario Number Two: A U.S.-China War

It is widely understood that the wars waged over the next century will not be fought to prove one country's power over another. Instead, they will be waged over land and its valuable natural resources, such as oil, water, and its potential use for growing grains and other food. It has been predicted that a potential war between the United States and China will be over goods.

Jed Babbin's book *Showdown: Why China Wants War with the United States*, argues that China is looking to pick

Wal-Mart is a significant trading partner with China. If Wal-Mart decides not to sell Chinese-made products—trade worth more than $18 billion a year—it could lead to job loss and unemployment throughout China.

a fight with the United States, which is still regarded as the world's remaining superpower. *Showdown* predicts the ways in which a war between the two nations might play out in scenarios that read more like a thrilling Hollywood movie script and less like anything that might actually occur in real life.

Some of the book's scenarios include China's push for superpower status on the world stage; the potential for China to wage a nuclear attack on the United States and engage in cyber warfare; and China's growing economic clout and obsession with oil-rich nations, which could upset America's supply of oil. Most of these scenarios are unlikely to occur. China may have a growing military, but it is not yet strong enough to launch a large-scale attack on a country with as rich a military history as the United States.

However, China's growing economy is a factor that definitely deserves attention. With its low labor standards, the country has stolen jobs away from the United States and has exported its products overseas at unfairly high prices. In truth, the jobs that China has taken away from U.S. workers are jobs that are designed for an unskilled and uneducated workforce. They are mostly seen as jobs that the American workforce is uninterested in doing. Also, more than 60 percent of Chinese exports to the United States are produced by firms owned by foreign companies, many of them American. These companies moved their operations overseas in response to competitive pressures to lower production costs, which creates lower prices for consumers. America has a number of very large, very powerful companies that import goods to China. These companies, including Wal-Mart and Hallmark, have the power to force Chinese suppliers to keep their costs as low as possible. Wal-Mart alone purchased $18 billion worth of Chinese goods in 2004, making it China's eighth largest trading partner—ahead of Australia, Canada, and Russia.

So the likelihood of China waging war on the United States is low. It is too dependent on the United States and its companies for goods and services. If any disaster occurs, we are likely to see China become a stronger financial partner to the United States.

Hollywood Loves Doomsday Movies

Hollywood, the moviemaking capital of the world, has long seen doomsday scenarios as perfect and sensational endings to a world created for the silver screen. Hundreds of doomsday-themed movies exist, but the top six are:

- *Waterworld*: Global warming causes the complete melting of glaciers and polar ice caps, nearly flooding the entire planet.
- *The Terminator* and *The Matrix*: Computers unite to create one supercomputer that has super intelligence and is on a mission to destroy humanity.
- *Blindness*: The entire population, except for one woman, goes blind almost instantly. Mass hysteria breaks out, quarantines are ineffective, and the strong and brutal hoard food and commit atrocities.
- *Children of Men*: Women are unable to have children and the cause is unknown, leaving the world's population unable to reproduce. This leads to the extinction of the human race.
- *Armageddon*: A huge asteroid threatens to strike Earth, wiping out every single living thing on the planet.

Scenario Number Three: Terrorism

Put simply, terrorism is any act that is intended to create fear in a deliberate target. On September 11, 2001, a terrorist organization attacked the United States. Over the course of just a few hours, there was a massive loss of life, significant disruption to our financial system, and widespread fear. But terrorism comes in many forms. There is political, religious, and civil terrorism. And there is a fourth type of terrorism that is growing: cyberterrorism.

Cyberterrorism is the use of computers and information, particularly through the Internet, to cause physical harm or the severe disruption of infrastructure in society. Terrorists could target computer networks that are critical to our nation's power supplies, telecommunications, and financial systems, and wreak havoc on the country.

The threat of cyberterrorism has grabbed the attention of the mass media, the security community, and the computer and information technology industry. Journalists, politicians, and experts in a variety of fields have created elaborate scenarios in which sophisticated cyberterrorists hack into computers and gain control of our government, military, air traffic control, and financial systems to wreck havoc and endanger the

Computers control our nation's entire infrastructure, from financial transactions and security to traffic patterns in major cities. The collapse of our computer networking systems could lead to worldwide panic.

lives of millions of people while creating a massive national security risk.

The potential threat of a cyberterrorist attack is terrifying. Yet despite the predictions and fear surrounding this type of attack, there has been no single recorded incident of real cyberterrorism. However, there have been mock demonstrations that have shown us just how susceptible we are to cyberterrorist attacks. So how safe are our financial systems from a cyber attack?

Consider that on November 9, 2001, just two months after the 9/11 terrorist attacks, two postgraduate students at Cambridge University in the United Kingdom announced that they had cracked a financial computer system used by banks and credit card companies around the world. The system was created to secure the personal identification numbers of customers' accounts. The students were able to crack IBM's 4758, a device that encrypts account numbers in order to make financial transactions secure. In 1998, the system was deemed compliant with the highest level of cryptography security standards by U.S. federal authorities. The system is used worldwide, including by the U.S. Treasury Department, which uses the system to sell bonds and treasury bills to the public over the Internet.

Fortunately, the students didn't steal anyone's money. Instead, they said they conducted the hack to show that the computer programs in place to protect the world's financial

With the world growing ever more dependent on computers and technology, any tampering with these systems could have devastating consequences.

systems aren't as secure as originally thought. Electronic transactions—which include everything from tuition payments, direct deposit of paychecks, store purchases made by debit cards, online purchases, and the buying and selling of stocks and bonds—accounted for 49.5 billion transactions totaling an impressive $695 trillion. The students proved that the interconnected nature of the world's financial systems, which move billions of dollars around the world each day, are only as strong as the weakest link.

Since these students' attack on the world's financial computer systems, new guidelines have been put into place to establish the type of encryption and security measures necessary to safeguard money and assets in the event of a cyber attack. The U.S. Office of Homeland Security, which was created after 9/11, works to establish these guidelines with the help of today's leading scholars on computing, network security, and cyber infrastructure.

Chapter 4

PREVENTING AN ECONOMIC MELTDOWN

Christopher Dodd, the chairman of the U.S. Senate's Banking, Housing and Urban Affairs Committee, delivers opening remarks during a hearing for a proposed bailout of the U.S. auto industry.

So far, we've looked at financial doomsday scenarios from a few different perspectives. We've looked at scenarios that could happen and ones that seem more like the plot of a Hollywood movie. We've examined these scenarios to determine if they pose real threats, and we've seen the potential consequences of a financial meltdown. We've scrutinized the possibility of these scenarios ever becoming real—and why they likely won't. Now let's look at what is being done to

Tips on How to Survive a Global Financial Meltdown

1. Keep cash on hand. The moment you see banks beginning to fail, it's likely you'll be in serious trouble if you have more than the government insures. The best way to protect yourself is to keep a cash reserve. In an absolute worst-case scenario, cash could become worthless. But in most cases, it will save you. If you have extensive savings, consider keeping a portion of it at home or somewhere else safe.

2. Stockpile food. It may sound crazy, but just think about what happens when the news predicts a major snowstorm or hurricane: there is always a rush on food at the grocery store as people stock up. The same kind of preparation might help you in a financial meltdown, too. It pays to have a few days' worth of food handy, particularly prepackaged food

Amid stock market crashes and rising unemployment, people tend to stockpile food in case the supply runs low or prices rise to unaffordable levels.

that doesn't require cooking. A major meltdown to our financial system, a terrorist attack, or a cyber attack could mean the disruption of power supplies, which will immediately affect perishable foods at the grocery store.

3. Be prepared for job loss. Financial advisors always suggest keeping a minimum of three to six months of living expenses in an emergency savings account in case you lose your job. In the event of a major financial collapse, few industries will be spared and your job could be at risk. Being prepared with a few months' worth of living expenses will enable you to cover your mortgage or rent, food, utilities, debt payments, and other expenses that you can't put off even in an emergency.

make sure that these financial doomsday scenarios never become a reality.

Government Bailouts

Whenever the financial services industry faced severe problems in the past, the U.S. government got involved by providing the industry with bailouts to help steady the economy before a major collapse occurred. A bailout is when a government loans or gives money to a failing business to save it from bankruptcy or collapse. The federal government has been bailing out companies for decades to keep people employed and avoid economic trouble. In the 1970s, it gave a substantial financial life raft to Lockheed, a company engaged in the research, development, and manufacture of advanced technology systems, products, and services. The company's failure would have meant significant job loss for the people of California, where the company was headquartered, as well as a significant impact on America's national defense.

Similarly, the federal government stepped in when the 9/11 terrorist attacks crippled the U.S. airline industry, which was already financially troubled. After the attacks, the government grounded all airlines until it could sort out what exactly occurred. Grounding the airlines caused massive financial strain on the industry, so the government signed into law the Air Transportation Safety and Stabilization Act. The act compensated airlines for their financial loss and was intended to keep the industry afloat in a time when people were afraid of flying.

Some financial experts are concerned that when the government moves to bail out ailing companies or industries, it is really keeping the financial crisis from reaching rock bottom, thus delaying the economy's natural recovery process. Others believe that government bailouts are necessary to help the economy calm down and help assets stabilize in value. When the economy is unhinged, people don't know the real value of their assets, what homes are really worth, and what investment banks are worth. This can cause economic paralysis, in which people are too fearful to spend any money, thus creating no movement in the economy. Government bailouts help motivate the economy and create a sense of calm that encourages people to spend, thus boosting the economy. In addition to the airline industry, the federal government has also bailed out banks, the auto industry, the financial services industry, and even the city of New York when it fell on hard times.

Changes in Consumer Behavior

In a recent Gallup poll, which measures public opinion, Americans were asked to list the possible ways in which families could cope with the rising prices that occur during a financial crisis. In response, 81 percent reported that they would make more of an effort to find cheaper prices for the products they buy. Three out of four said they would spend less on entertainment, recreation, and eating out. More than half of the poll's respondents said they would either create a monthly budget or make a greater effort to stick to the one they have.

Consumer behavior affects more than just the American financial system. Goods and services purchased by Americans make up one-fifth of the global economy. When spending is good, Americans buy more goods and services. That translates into jobs and economic growth around the world. But when the economy is bad and spending decreases as a result, economies around the world feel the pinch.

If consumers don't spend at all during a difficult economic time, the potential for the economy to worsen increases. Attitudes toward consumer spending are difficult to change. We have to start saving a little more but must continue to spend to see the economy change direction.

When a financial crisis strikes, retailers are among the first to feel the immediate aftershocks. When people begin to struggle to pay their credit cards, basic household expenses,

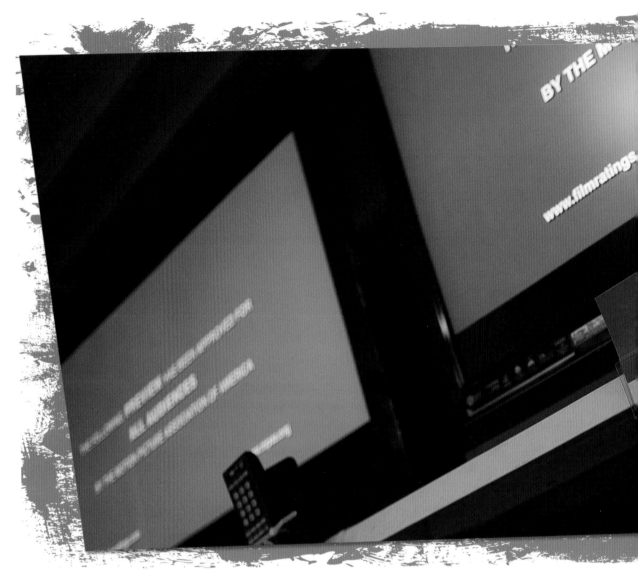

When the economy does poorly, expensive products, such as flat-screen televisions and digital cameras, sit on store shelves unsold.

and mortgages, they are often not out shopping for new plasma-screen televisions, cars, or expensive clothes. But these purchases, even the small ones—such as CDs, DVDs, movie tickets, and dinner out—help keep the economy moving.

New Regulations for the Financial Services Industry

In 2008, the financial industry nearly collapsed under the weight of deregulation imposed a decade earlier. Once highly regulated, the banking industry had no watchdog. Among the widespread abuses committed by banks were off-the-books accounting to hide losses and debt; offering investment, commercial banking, and insurance services that proved to be a conflict of interest; and loaning to those who were not able to pay the money back.

Another problem was that banks and other financial institutions were not required to be open and honest to the government about what they were doing and how bad their debt really was. Because the U.S. financial system is global—meaning that American banks do business with British, Chinese, and Japanese banks and other banks around the world—the United States is now forced to lead an international effort to find out where these bad investments are in other nations' banks. Understanding the full scale of the problem is the only way to find regulations that work for both the U.S. financial system and the global marketplace. Establishing regulations worldwide will take a lot of cooperation from countries around the world.

As a result, there are now new regulations that monitor banks and other financial institutions. As the economy rights itself in 2009 and beyond, people will see more rules and regulations put in place to safeguard their money and investments, and to prevent continued abuse of the financial services industry.

Computer Security

"There is no such thing as a totally secure system," says Kevin Mitnick, who has the distinction of being in the *Guinness Book of World Records* as the world's most notorious hacker. Mitnick spent nearly five years in jail for seven software felonies involving hacking. "All it takes is one vulnerability to compromise an entire system," he says.

Avoiding these vulnerabilities is the job of security firms like Digital Defense, which performs security assessments for financial companies. Many financial institutions provide electronic connectivity from their networks to payment networks like Fedwire. Fedwire is a money transfer system set up by the Federal Reserve Bank. It is the primary U.S. financial computer network.

It's these connections that pose the greatest risk. Hackers are not likely to go after Citibank, Wells Fargo, or any other major banking institution that has the most secure, up-to-date software and security programs available. Instead, they're going to go after a small, local bank that might work with Fedwire. It's probable that smaller banks will not have extensive computer security systems that monitor network security. This will make it possible for hackers to gain access to the system through the Internet, gain administrative

Pierre Kroma, an IT security consultant, successfully hacks a Web server to demonstrate how vulnerable computer networks can be.

control of an inside computer with access to one of these payment networks, and launch the attack.

With cyberterrorism becoming more of a potential threat, the U.S. government added personnel to the Office of Homeland Security to help monitor this area of concern. Former president George W. Bush appointed a special White House adviser for cyberspace security to keep both the president's office and the public apprised of computer security–related issues and developments. This adviser also works with the National Security Council, which advises the president on national security and foreign policies. The council also serves as the president's principal arm for coordinating policies among various government agencies.

A Cyclical Process

As explained in chapter 1, the economy is cyclical, which means that it has its natural ups and downs. There will always be times of expansion, when the economy is growing, businesses are doing well, employment is high, and people are making good money and are out spending it on products and services, vacations, and gifts. There will also be times when the economy is not doing so well, when spending declines, business production slows, and workers are laid off. The economy often corrects itself by moving through the economic cycle, and it usually emerges stronger than ever before.

asset An item of value, such as a home, stocks, investments, etc.

bailout Monetary aid from the federal government given to banks and other institutions to help these institutions cover their loans, debts, and other costs of operation.

cryptography The act of enciphering and deciphering coded messages.

dollar The currency of the United States; issued by the U.S. Federal Reserve, it is the most traded currency in the world.

dot-com A company that does the majority of its business on the Internet.

encryption The process of transforming information to make it unreadable.

euro The currency of the European Union that was introduced to the global financial market in 1999; it is the second most traded currency in the world after the U.S. dollar.

franc The franc was the currency of France until the euro was introduced in 1999. However, it is still used in Switzerland, and the Swiss franc is a major world currency.

global pandemic An event occurring over a wide geographic area that affects an exceptionally high proportion of the population.

gross domestic product Also known as GDP, it is one measure of national income and output for a given country's economy; it is the total value of all final goods and services produced in a particular economy.

industrialized world A term used to describe a select group of countries that is highly developed.

inflation A rise in the general level of prices of goods and services in an economy over a period of time.

interest rate The price that a borrower pays for the use of money that he or she does not own.

manufacturing The use of machines, tools, and labor to make things for use or sale.

Mayan A term that refers to the indigenous peoples of parts of Mexico and Central America, and their culture, language, and history.

network A group of interconnected computers.

portfolio A mixture of investments held by either a financial institution or a private citizen.

pound The form of currency used in England.

program trading The use of computers to perform rapid sales of stock.

sorghum A term that refers to numerous species of grasses, some of which are raised for grain.

stock In business and finance, a share of stock means a portion of ownership in a corporation or company.

telecommunications The assisted transmission of signals over a distance for the purpose of communication.

Wall Street Located in New York City, it is a geographic neighborhood that forms the center of the U.S. financial services industry.

yen The form of currency used in Japan; it is the third most traded currency in the global financial market, after the U.S. dollar and the euro.

yuan The form of currency used in China.

American Finance Association
Haas School of Business
University of California
Berkeley, CA 94729-1900
(800) 835-6770
Web site: http://www.afajof.org
The American Finance Association is the premier academic
   organization devoted to the study and promotion of
   knowledge on financial economics.

Canadian Society for Industrial Security
P.O. Box 57006, Jackson Station
2 King Street West
Hamilton, ON L8P 4W9
Canada
(905) 853-6523
Web site: http://www.csis-scsi.org
The Canadian Society for Industrial Security is an association
   for professionals in the fields of computer and network
   security in Canada.

Computer Security Institute
11 West 19th Street, 3rd Floor
New York, NY 10011
(212) 600-3026
Web site: http://www.gocsi.com
The Computer Security Institute serves the needs of information technology and computer security professionals by
   offering membership, educational events, security sur-
   veys, tools, and resources.

Department of Homeland Security
U.S. Department of Homeland Security
Washington, DC 20528
(202) 282-8000
Web site: http://www.dhs.gov
The mission of the U.S. Department of Homeland Security is
    to lead a national effort to secure the United States and
    preserve the country's freedoms. The department also
    prepares for and responds to all hazards and disasters.

Harvard Business School
Soldier's Field
Boston, MA 02163
(617) 495-6000
Web site: http://www.hbs.edu
This is one of the leading business schools in the world.

Institute of Canadian Bankers
200 Wellington Street West, 15th Floor
Toronto, ON M5V 3C7
Canada
(866) 866-2601
Web site: https://www.icb.org/english/index.asp
Since the Institute of Canadian Bankers was established
    in 1970 as the Canadian Securities Institute, nearly
    three-quarters of a million financial professionals
    have completed their career training and development
    courses there.

National Security Council
The White House

1600 Pennsylvania Avenue NW
Washington, DC 20500
(202) 456-1111
Web site: http://www.whitehouse.gov/administration/eop/nsc
The National Security Council's main responsibility is to
   advise and assist the president of the United States on
   national security and foreign policy issues. The council
   also serves as the president's principal arm for coordinating these policies among various government agencies.

Web Sites

Due to the changing nature of Internet links, Rosen Publishing
has developed an online list of Web sites related to the subject
of this book. This site is updated regularly. Please use this
link to access the list:

http://www.rosenlinks.com/doom/fina

For Further Reading

Appleman, Dan. *Always Use Protection: A Teen's Guide to Safe Computing*. Berkeley, CA: Apress, 2009.

Barba, Rick. *The Doomsday Dust* (Spy Gear Adventures). New York, NY: Aladdin Publishing, 2006.

Blumenthal, Karen. *Six Days in October: The Stock Market Crash of 1929: A Wall Street Journal Book for Children*. New York, NY: Atheneum Books for Young Readers, 2002.

Box, Matthew J., and David M. Haugen. *Social Issues Firsthand—Terrorism*. Farmington Hills, MI: Greenhaven Press, 2005.

Donohoe, Helen. *Terrorism: A Look at the Way the World Is Today* (Issues of the World). Mankato, MN: Stargazer Books, 2005.

Fitch, Thomas P. *Career Opportunities in Banking, Finance, and Insurance*. New York, NY: Checkmark Books, 2007.

Frank, Mitch. *Understanding September 11th: Answering Questions About the Attacks on America*. New York, NY: Viking Juvenile, 2002.

Freedman, Russell. *Children of the Great Depression*. Boston, MA: Clarion Books, 2005.

Guyatt, Nicholas. *Have a Nice Doomsday: Why Millions of Americans Are Looking Forward to the End of the World*. New York, NY: Harper Perennial, 2007.

Kiyosaki, Robert T. *Rich Dad Poor Dad for Teens: The Secrets About Money—That You Don't Learn in School!* New York, NY: Little, Brown Young Readers, 2004.

Levy, Joel. *The Doomsday Book: Scenarios for the End of the World*. London, England: Vision Paperbacks, 2006.

McAlpine, Margaret. *Working in Banking and Finance*. Strongsville, OH: Gareth Stevens Publishing, 2005.

Miller, Debra A. *Importing from China*. Farmington Hills, MI: Greenhaven Press, 2009.

Moran, Richard. *Doomsday: End-of-the-World Scenarios*. Exton, PA: Alpha Publishing, 2002.

Moyers, Bill. *Welcome to Doomsday*. New York, NY: New York Review Books Collection, 2006.

Newman, Matthew. *You Have Mail: True Stories of Cybercrime* (24/7: Science Behind the Scenes). San Francisco, CA: Children's Press, 2007.

Page Harman, Hollis. *Money Sense for Kids*. Hauppauge, NY: Barron's Educational Series, 2005

Robbins, David. *Endworld: Doomsday*. Wayne, PA: Leisure Books, 2009.

Snedden, Robert. *Ancient China* (Technology in Times Past). Collingwood, Ontario: Saunders Book Co., 2009.

Stanat, Michael. *China's Generation Y: Understanding the Future Leaders of the World's Next Superpower*. Paramus, NJ: Homa & Sekey Books, 2005.

Weber, Sandra, and Shanly Dixon. *Growing Up Online: Young People and Digital Technologies*. New York, NY: Palgrave Macmillan, 2007.

White, Jonathan R. *Terrorism and Homeland Security: An Introduction*. Florence, KY: Wadsworth Publishing, 2008.

World Bank. *Getting to Know the World Bank: A Guide for Young People*. Washington, DC: World Bank Publications, 2005.

Bibliography

BBC News. "Doomsday Fears of Terror Cyber-attacks."
October 11, 2001. Retrieved February 27, 2009 (http://
news.bbc.co.uk/1/hi/sci/tech/1593018.stm).

Colvin, Geoff. "The Anti-Doomsday Scenario." CNN.com,
June 25, 2008. Retrieved February 19, 2009 (http://
money.cnn.com/2008/06/24/news/economy/colvin_
recovery.fortune/index.htm).

Francis, David R. "Recession Is a Given. Can We Avoid
Depression?" *Christian Science Monitor*, March 24, 2008.
Retrieved February 18, 2009 (http://www.csmonitor.com/
2008/0324/p17s02-wmgn.html?page=10).

Gaffen, David. "Betting Against the Doomsday Scenario." *Wall
Street Journal*, January 30, 2009. Retrieved February 19,
2009 (http://blogs.wsj.com/marketbeat/2009/01/30/
betting-against-the-doomsday-scenario).

Hawver, Joe. "Global Financial Meltdown Is a Simple Matter
of Information Asymmetry." MLive.com, January 5, 2009.
Retrieved February 26, 2009 (http://www.mlive.com/
opinion/kalamazoo/index.ssf/2009/01/global_financial_
meltdown_is_a.html).

Inquisitir. "Basic Tips on Surviving a Global Financial
Meltdown." September 25, 2008. Retrieved February 22,
2009 (http://www.inquisitr.com/3935/basic-tips-on-
surviving-a-global-financial-meltdown).

Michaels, Adrian. "This Financial Crisis Is Now Truly Global."
Telegraph (UK), February 20, 2009. Retrieved February 22,
2009 (http://www.telegraph.co.uk/finance/financetopics/
financialcrisis/4736387/This-financial-crisis-is-now-
truly-global.html).

Nelson, Cary, ed. "The Great Depression." University of Illinois at Urbana-Champaign, 2009. Retrieved February 22, 2009 (http://www.english.illinois.edu/maps/depression/depression.htm).

Newser. "4 Financial Doomsday Scenarios." December 17, 2008. Retrieved February 22, 2009 (http://www.newser.com/story/45591/4-financial-doomsday-scenarios.html).

Post, Charlie. "Their Crisis, Our Consequences." International Viewpoint, October 2008. Retrieved February 23, 2009 (http://www.internationalviewpoint.org/spip.php?article1540).

Pravda. "China Makes U.S. Economy Its Hostage." October 10, 2007. Retrieved February 27, 2009 (http://english.pravda.ru/business/finance/99414-0).

Pritchard, Carolyn. "Cracks in the System." New World, 2009. Retrieved February 21, 2009 (http://journalism.berkeley.edu/ngno/reports/newworld/cyberterrorism.html).

Sands, David R. "Financial Crisis Reshapes World Order." InfoWars.com, October 12, 2008. Retrieved February 22, 2009 (http://www.infowars.com/financial-crisis-reshapes-world-order).

Shapiro, Robert. "Al-Qaida and the GDP: How Much Would Terrorism Damage the U.S. Economy? Less Than You'd Expect." Slate.com, February 28, 2003. Retrieved February 24, 2009 (http://www.slate.com/id/2079298).

Stopsky, Fred. "Doomsday Scenario-China-U.S. War." *The Impudent Observer*, January 22, 2008. Retrieved February 25, 2009 (http://theimpudentobserver.com/world-news/doomsday-scenario-china-us-war).

Weimann, Gabriel. "Cyberterrorism: How Real Is the Threat?" U.S. Institute of Peace, December 2004. Retrieved April 10, 2009 (http://www.usip.org/pubs/specialreports/sr119.html).

Index

About the Author

Laura La Bella is a writer and editor living in Rochester, New York. Among her books, La Bella has profiled actress and activist Angelina Jolie in *Angelina Jolie: Goodwill Ambassador to the UN*; reported on the declining availability of the world fresh water supply in *Not Enough to Drink: Pollution, Drought, and Tainted Water Supplies*; and has examined the food industry in *Safety and the Food Supply*.

Photo Credits

Cover, pp. 1, 4–5 Spencer Platt/Getty Images; pp. 7, 13, 22–23, 24–25, 30, 33, 44, 51 © AP Images; p. 11 FPG/Hulton Archive/Getty Images; pp. 16–17 © www.istockphoto.com/Nikada; pp. 18, 38–39 Shutterstock.com; pp. 20–21 Sebastian Derungs/AFP/Getty Images; pp. 28–29 Al Rai Al Aam/Feature Story News/Getty Images; pp. 34–35 © culliganphoto/Alamy; pp. 40–41 © www.istockphoto.com/Rich Yasick; p. 43 Chip Somodevilla/Getty Images; pp. 48–49 Jim Watson/AFP/Getty Images.

Designer: Sam Zavieh; Editor: Nicholas Croce;
Photo Researcher: Amy Feinberg